CRYSTALS FOR BEGINNERS

Jacqueline French

The Essential Guide to the Power of Crystals for Happiness, Love and Wellbeing

First published in 2019 by Erin Rose Publishing

Design: Julie Anson

ISBN: 978-1-9161523-2-8

A CIP record for this book is available from the British Library.

DISCLAIMER: This book is for informational purposes only and not intended as a substitute for the medical advice. If you have a health issue, you should consult your doctor or healthcare professional for diagnosis or treatment The reader should consult a physician in all matters relating to his/her health, and particularly with respect to any symptoms that may require medical attention.

The descriptions of the crystal healing, their qualities and benefits are for informational purposes and do not guarantee effects, nor is this book or the information it contains intended as medical advice or diagnosis. Crystals healing does not offer a cure. All illnesses and diseases must be seen by your doctor for diagnosis and treatment of any health concerns. No warranty may be created by the advice contained herein may not be suitable for every person or situation.

Crystals are only to be used as a compliment to medical care and other complimentary therapies. You can make complementary healing part of a complete health care programme. The healing properties of crystals and stones, in this book are based on our own experiences, research and beliefs. No recommendation is made for specific individual and qualified professional advice must be sought. The healing attributes and benefits of the crystals and stones in this book are experienced differently by individuals and this does not mean you will benefit or experience changes as described within.

The definitions and descriptions in this book are education and insight in crystals and crystal healing. Crystal healing is a complementary therapy which should be carried out by a suitably qualified crystal healing practitioner. The author and publisher fully disclaim responsibility for any adverse effects that may arise.

CONTENTS

INTRODUCTION

Welcome To Essential Crystals for Beginners!

Beautiful crystals, gemstones and semi-precious stones have been used in many cultures throughout history for their healing attributes to energise, protect, transform and bring good fortune. In this book, you can discover how to use the natural magic of crystals for your everyday wellbeing.

The intriguing energy of each stone offers beneficial qualities and we are intuitively drawn to crystals which resonate with us. Choosing and working with crystals is a journey of self-discovery and you might begin to wonder if you choose the crystal or does the crystal choose you?

Crystals are used to improve the energy flow of the body and mind, for success, vitality, healing and wellbeing. They are often used for specific purposes, such as courage, love, confidence, peace, clarity, relaxation and motivation. Improvements occur when crystal energies interact with our energy field so they are worn on the body or placed around the home to enhance the environment.

You can carry an energising crystal in your purse for more money and prosperity or place a calming crystal under your pillow for a better night's sleep. You can use crystals and minerals to calm your mind and improve your mood. A Himalayan salt lamp gives out a lovely warm glow and it can be used to improve the air in your home and create a better atmosphere.

Crystals are not only beautiful, they amplify, cleanse and absorb energy, which enhances your space and there are so many shapes and types. You can choose quartz points, tumble stones, jewellery, sparkly geodes, or perhaps carved crystal angels, animals or pyramids appeal to you. If you have an attraction to a certain stone, you often find it's the right stone for you.

The size of a crystal doesn't always reflect its strength and working consistently with them will intensify their benefits as your energy interacts with them. Have fun and be a positive influence when enjoying your stones. Crystals rock!

The Power of Crystals

Gemstones, crystals and semi-precious stones have always been sought after for their attributes and beauty. Crystals have sometimes been dismissed as a hippy fashion accessory but they are so much more than that. Using the power of crystals can benefit our self-care and wellbeing in everyday life.

In our modern world, crystals are often used to enhance happiness and wellness. They are now in mainstream popularity for life enhancement, personal growth and living your best life. Although there is scepticism around their benefits, they are often used in meditation or worn to improve emotional wellbeing. You can try it and see. If it works for you, and it does for many, that's great!

Gemstones have been associated with mysticism, used by seers, shamans, wise women and healers for their special vibrations and natural magic. When old techniques survive for millennia, they do so with credibility. For centuries the unique attributes of gemstones has been associated with astrology and some were identified as zodiac birth stones. Crystals are a direct connection to the earth and its healing energy.

In a fast paced world which distracts us from our needs, we're rediscovering who we are and taking charge of our own health and happiness.

Crystals are frequently used in meditation, mindfulness and healing therapies like reiki and massage, for focusing, amplifying, absorbing and holding energy. There's also the practical application of crystals in electrical devices too.

Quartz crystals are piezoelectric which means an electrical charge accumulates in them. Marcel Vogel, an IBM scientist, who invented the magnetic coating used in disc drives, contributed to the development of liquid crystal displays (LCD). These are widely used to generate a high frequency charge in the use of electronic devices and watches.

This eminent scientist later created 'Vogel crystals' which are crystals that are cut to a very precise specification which he used for therapeutic healing benefits. Vogel taught how life force energy can be amplified through the crystals and he pledged to replace their mysticism with knowledge. He went on to focus on human-plant communication and became known as a spiritual scientist.

Crystals work by interacting with energy fields, particularly the body's energy field and the chakra system. This interaction can benefit us depending on the attributes of the crystal and our intention for using it. Your intention is so important.

Know that you have within you, the power to attract, create and manifest what you ask for – also known as the Law of Attraction. You can use the power of your thoughts to direct energy between yourself and your crystal. Crystals are energetic tools for you to use, with the direction and focus of your own energy which is so much stronger than you may believe.

When you are working with crystals, you charge and magnify the crystals energy for positive transformation. Whether you are seeking confidence, prosperity or protection, it's your focused intention which activates the attributes of the crystal. Crystals are tools for you to use for change. It's you who uses intention to harness the crystals qualities.

The Power of Intention

The most important thing to remember is…

INTENTION IS EVERYTHING!

Focus clearly on what you want to use the crystal for. Sabotaging beliefs like low self-esteem can make you doubt how capable of this you actually are but believe in yourself. Crystals hold an innate, unique power but so do you! So please don't invest in the belief that the crystal will solve every issue in your life. It's teamwork. You still need to take action. Intention, focus and action used together are an unstoppable force.

Programming Your Crystals

Programming your crystal is a commonly used term for setting your intention. Some say crystals also need to be charged but setting your intention will activate and energise your crystal which already vibrates at a particular frequency. You can boost it further if you wish, using the same methods for cleansing – just adjust your intention. Setting your intention involves firmly stating your intention and visualising your desired outcome. Below are two ways of programming your crystal with your intention. Use whichever appeals to you or experiment with them to find what works best for you.

1. Visualisation Method To Program Your Crystal

All you have to do is close your eyes, hold the crystal and visualise the existence of what you wish for, with as much believe, trust and concentration you can muster. Hold the vision for a few minutes. The longer you hold the image of your desire the better.

2. Method To Program Your Crystal

Focus on your feet in contact with the ground and sit quietly for a few minutes.

- *Choose an intention which is the best possible outcome you can imagine, which has integrity and is good for everyone concerned.*
- *Hold the crystal in your hand and be aware of how it feels.*
- *Bring your attention to your third eye chakra at the centre of your forehead and hold your intention here for a few minutes.*
- *Next bring your attention to your root chakra at the centre of your pelvis and hold your intention here for a few minutes. This begins to move your energy into stronger form.*
- *Then firmly and slowly state the following affirmation:*

I am content.
I have everything I need.
I am no longer challenged.
I have everything I need and require.
Everything is part of me. I am secure.
I am content and peaceful.

This process can quickly align your intention with the reality and contentment of having your desired outcome.

Keeping an amethyst for the third eye chakra and garnet for the root chakra close by during this meditation will give your intention an extra boost.

Choosing Crystals

You can choose crystals according to their specific attributes such as strength, balance or courage. Or you can pick crystals according to which chakras you wish to work with or use your instincts and pick ones which you are drawn to. If a crystal catches your eye, pay close attention to how it makes you feel. Hold the crystal if you can. Perhaps you feel calmer, lighter or more energised when you touch it. You can try several and compare what you feel. Often, your first impression is the correct one, so trust your gut. A great experiment is to choose a crystal which you really like, then later look up your crystal's attributes. You usually find that it's completely appropriate for you which helps you to understand yourself better.

Zodiac Birthstones

20 Jan – 19 Feb	*Aquarius*	*Garnet*	*Protection*
19 Feb – 21 Mar	*Pisces*	*Amethyst*	*Wisdom*
21 Mar – 20 Apr	*Aries*	*Bloodstone*	*Enthusiasm*
20 Apr – 21 May	*Taurus*	*Sapphire*	*Patience*
21 May – 21 Jun	*Gemini*	*Agate*	*Versatility*
21 Jun – 23 Jul	*Cancer*	*Emerald*	*Love*
23 Jul – 23 Aug	*Leo*	*Onyx*	*Generosity*
23 Aug – 23 Sep	*Virgo*	*Carnelian*	*Confidence*
23 Sep – 23 Oct	*Libra*	*Peridot*	*Charm*
23 Oct – 22 Nov	*Scorpio*	*Beryl*	*Determination*
22 Nov – 22 Dec	*Sagittarius*	*Citrine*	*Optimism*
22 Dec – 20 Jan	*Capricorn*	*Ruby*	*Ambition*

Astrological birthstones are the original birthstones which have been around since ancient times.They are different to modern birthstones which were assigned by jewellers in 1912. Zodiac birthstones were thought to bring out your natural abilities and bring good luck, but its best to choose a stone you have a connection with.

Cleansing Your Crystals

When you get new stones, always cleanse them to remove any residual energy from them. Crystals can be cleansed in several ways. Whichever method you choose, hold a clear intention that the crystal is cleansed of all previous energies. The methods below will cleanse your crystals and some will charge them too.

- *Rinse the crystal under a flow of water or wash it in salted water and then gently dry it. This works well for quartz crystals; rose, smoky and clear quartz, amethyst and aventurine. Avoid prolonged water contact with softer, water soluble crystals like turquoise, lapis lazuli, moonstone, topaz, malachite, kyanite, calcite, selenite or any crystals ending in 'ite'.*
- *Leaving your crystal in moonlight or even out-doors overnight can also charge your crystal. Sunlight can also work but be careful of strong sun as this can be a fire risk.*
- *You can cleanse crystals by placing them near a Himalayan salt lamp, which will energise as well as clear them.*
- *A Native American way of cleansing crystals is to use dried sage smoke or a smudge stick and allow the smoke to drift over them.*
- *Placing smaller crystals onto a large quartz geode will clear and energise them.*

How To Use Your Crystals

Crystals are available in natural points, tumble stones, slices, clusters, polished points, spheres, pyramids, geodes and an infinite number of carved shapes and animals. There are so many ways to use crystals and getting creative with them is great fun.

- *They can be worn as jewellery, held or kept close during meditation.*
- *Hold one in your palm as you fall asleep or you can put one under your pillow.*
- *You can keep a crystal with a gratitude journal for communication and appreciation.*
- *They can be programmed for a specific purpose; healing, manifesting or good luck.*
- *Crystals can be placed on the body for chakra balancing.*
- *They can be used as pendulums for dowsing.*
- *You can make crystal water, also known as crystal 'elixir'.*
- *Crystals can be placed around your home to improve the atmosphere.*
- *They can be placed around your garden or scattered around the environment.*
- *You can make a beautiful crystal grid with a specific healing focus.*
- *They can be kept in your pocket or purse to attract prosperity.*
- *Placed on or around the body for healing.*
- *A selenite wand or clear quartz can cleanse the aura and other crystals.*
- *They can be used during reiki treatments or massages, held or kept close by.*
- *You can display crystals for decoration or a table centrepiece.*
- *You can create a thoughtful gift. Choose some relevant crystals and place them in a lovely drawstring bag for weddings, birthdays, going-away-presents, starting university, moving house or beginning a new job.*
- *Crystal gardens make a beautiful table display. You can combine succulents or air plants, flower petals or moss, in a decorative bowl with a few well placed crystals.*

Mindfulness, Meditation and Personal Space

Meditation and mindfulness calms the body, reduces stress, promotes emotional health and boosts self-awareness. It's one of the best self-care techniques and it has so many benefits. Meditations don't need to be long and complicated. If you only have 5 or 10 minutes you can just sit quietly being aware of the present moment.

Dedicate a space in your home where you can relax and feel good. If you only have space for a shelf, that will do. You can fill it with crystals, plants, candles, pictures or photographs. It's your space to keep your favourite things where you can quietly reflect, be mindful and meditate. Creating a peaceful, positive uplifting space is great for self-care and improving your mood.

Aura Brushing

If you are feeling stressed or distracted, try moving a piece of selenite over the whole body, holding it a few inches off the skin, starting with the head and working your way down with outward sweeping movements. Selenite calms and absorbs unpleasant vibrations, so it's soothing. This kind of 'aura brushing' can be done daily or whenever you feel like it. It only needs to take 2 minutes and you'll feel refreshed afterwards.

How to Make a Crystal Grid

Crystal grids are great fun to make and can be used for healing, manifesting or whatever you wish. Trusting your intuition and having focused intention is the key, other than that there is no right or wrong.

1. *Choose a place to set up your grid where it won't be disturbed. You can create your grid on a cloth or paper but it's not necessary. A plain surface will do.*
2. *Firstly, set your intention. You can write this on paper or keep it in your mind as you create your grid. You can also place the paper in the centre of the grid.*
3. *Pick crystals which you are drawn to, or specifically for your purpose, for example; citrine for prosperity, rose quartz for love or obsidian for protection.*
4. *Decide what shape you want to use. You can use a piece of paper with a geometric shape drawn on it, make a spiral, circle, medicine wheel or your own original layout.*
5. *Focus on your intention and begin laying out your crystals, starting on the outside and working in towards the centre. Complete the grid with a centre stone. A quartz point is great for this but trust your intuition and what stones you are drawn to use.*
6. *Activate your crystal grid. Using a clear quartz point draw an invisible line joining one crystal to the next, again working from the outside in.*
7. *Leave your crystal grid in place for at least a month or more if you prefer. You can always return to it, amplifying it again with a quartz point and adding candles or clearing it with sage smoke if you wish.*

Crystal Elixirs

An easy way of benefitting from the crystal energies is to create crystal water, also known as crystal elixirs or essences.

Fill a jug with fresh filtered water or spring water. Choose a suitable clean crystal – amethyst, clear, smoky and rose quartz are ideal for this. You can choose other stones and add clear quartz to amplify the effects of the other crystals. You can choose several stones which suit your purpose and tailor-make crystal water.

You do need to be careful not to use certain crystals which could be potentially harmful if infused with water. The crystals azurite, malachite, pyrite and tiger's eye contain copper, iron, or lead and should **NOT** be used. If in doubt, stick to quartz which is usually easily identifiable.

Place the clean crystal in the water, cover it and allow it to infuse overnight or for at least an hour. You can use it for drinking, cooking and watering plants. Rose quartz elixir is a favourite for encouraging love and compassion and could be a useful one if you're cooking a meal for a loved one, or for Valentine's Day.

Chakra Balancing

The word chakra is actually an ancient Sanskrit word which means 'wheel'. Your body has 7 main chakras which are centres of life force energy which flows through every living thing. The 7 chakras are aligned along the spine. Each chakra centre has a particular vibration, colour and purpose, linking with the areas, organs and attributes of the body.

When chakras are strong and clear there is good physical, emotional and spiritual wellbeing. But if they become weak, overactive or blocked, our health and wellbeing suffers. The chakra energy system functions best when all of the chakras are balanced, not overactive or deficient, just working harmoniously together. Stress, trauma and disease all impact us negatively. But we can boost the flow of energy in the chakras and improve our wellbeing. Nourishing our whole body and mind with good nutrition, exercise, yoga, positive thinking, good self-care and being out in nature can all help.

You might be aware of particular areas of your body which don't feel right or you have recurrent problems in that area. Looking into the associations of the chakras can help you discover more about yourself and identify what you can do about it. Crystals resonate with particular chakras and some resonate with all of the chakras. They can be placed on the body, worn, used during meditation and complimentary therapies or you could see a reputable crystal healer for specialist advice.

The Seven Major Chakras

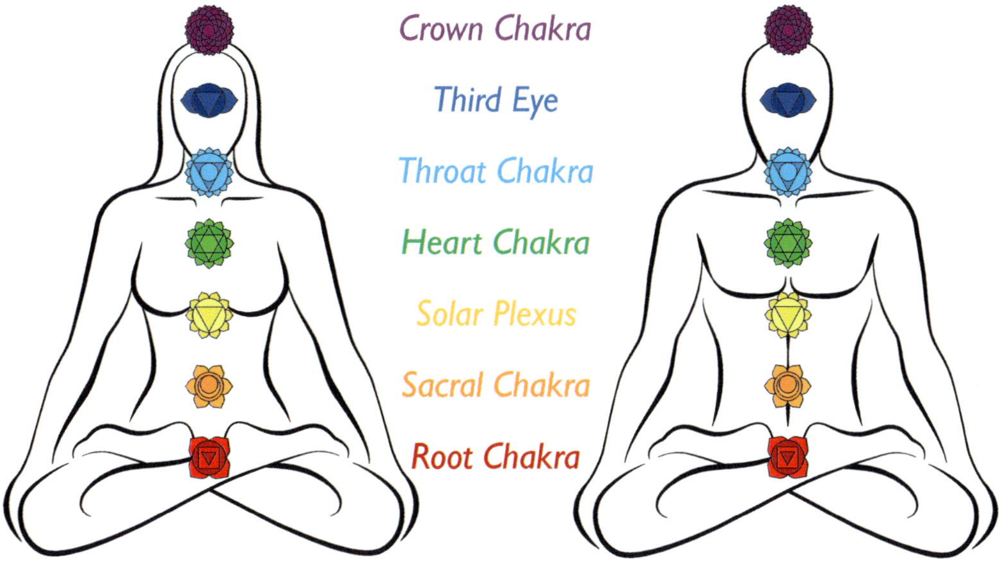

The 7 Chakras and Associations

Root Chakra – Security - Red

- ***Associations:*** *Survival, stability, family, trust, safety.*
- ***Physical:*** *Muscles, kidneys, skeleton, colon, hips, adrenals.*
- ***Imbalanced:*** *Insecurity, anger, anxiety, fears, tension, fatigue, constipation.*
- ***Beneficial crystals:*** *Red jasper, tiger's eye, smoky quartz, ruby, garnet, obsidian, tourmaline.*

Sacral Chakra – Emotions - Orange

- ***Associations:*** *Intimacy, pleasure, emotions, sexuality.*
- ***Physical:*** *Ovaries, testicles, bowel, bladder, intestines.*
- ***Imbalanced:*** *Addiction, guilt, criticism, frustration, low libido, fertility issues.*
- ***Beneficial crystals:*** *Carnelian, amber, sunstone, tiger's eye.*

Solar Plexus Chakra – Personal Power - Yellow

- ***Associations:*** *Confidence, mental function, vitality, power.*
- ***Physical:*** *Stomach, small intestine, pancreas, liver, gallbladder.*
- ***Imbalanced:*** *Controlling, timid, indecisive, fatigue, diabetes, arthritis.*
- ***Beneficial crystals:*** *Citrine, pyrite, golden topaz, yellow calcite.*

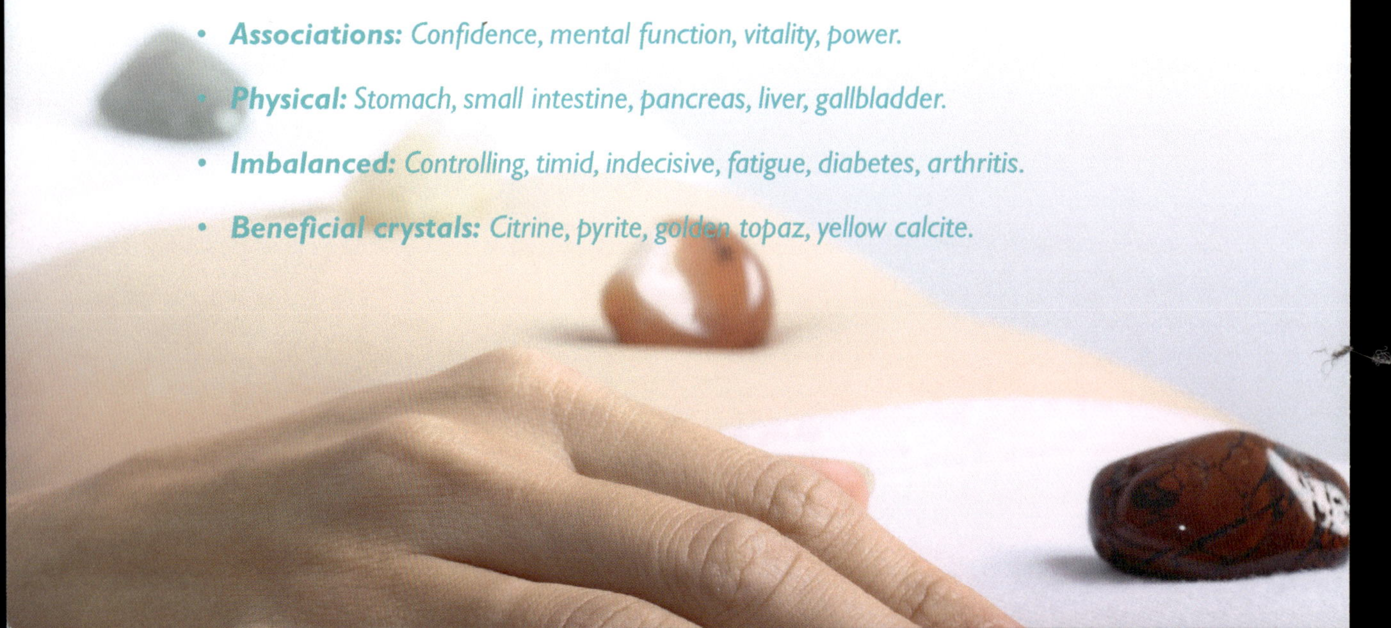

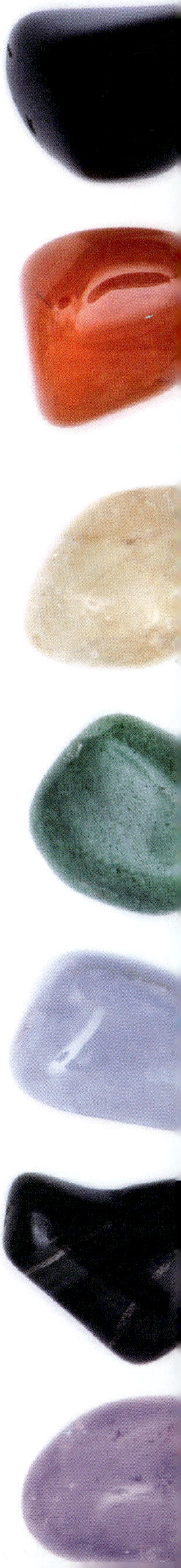

Heart Chakra – Love - Green (and pink)

- **Associations:** Love, relationships, compassion, joy.
- **Physical:** Heart, pericardium, circulation, thymus, blood pressure.
- **Imbalanced:** heartbreak, shock, defensiveness, jealously, apathy, panic.
- **Beneficial crystals:** Malachite, rose quartz, fluorite, rhodonite, aventurine.

Throat Chakra – Communication – Blue

- **Associations:** Expression, communication, creativity, honesty.
- **Physical:** Throat, oesophagus, neck, shoulders, lungs, thyroid, mouth.
- **Imbalanced:** Suppression, dishonesty, laryngitis, tonsillitis, neck pain.
- **Beneficial crystals:** Blue lace agate, turquoise, larimar, lapis lazuli.

Third Eye Chakra - Intuition – Indigo

- **Associations:** Foresight, clarity, intuition, psychic abilities.
- **Physical:** Eyes, nose, ears, memory, pituitary gland.
- **Imbalanced:** Insomnia, stress, visual problems, apathy, depression, anxiety.
- **Beneficial crystals:** Sodalite, kyanite, lapis lazuli, amethyst, labradorite.

Crown Chakra – Wisdom - Violet or white

- **Associations:** Purpose, spirituality, belonging, peace, wisdom.
- **Physical:** Head, brain, skeleton, nervous system, insomnia.
- **Imbalanced:** Isolation, apathy, loneliness, headaches, memory problems.
- **Beneficial crystals:** Amethyst, sugilite, clear quartz, howlite, selenite.

Remember, advice in this book is not a substitute for medical diagnosis and treatment and you must always seek your doctor's advice for any health issues you may be having.

Crystal Identifier

There is such a wide variety of crystals, it's impossible to fit them all into one book, so I've included popular, commonly used stones. You don't need to have a huge crystal collection. You can start with a few basics which will be a great foundation for working with crystals.

Some crystals come in many colours and in this section I have included the most commonly found colours. When choosing your crystals, you can bear in mind colours can be chosen according to chakras. For instance, agate is available in many colours so you can choose one which is most appropriate or whichever crystal you are drawn to.

Clear, smoky and rose quartz are an essential addition to any crystal collection. They are probably the most often used crystals for their amplifying and cleansing properties which can be used on their own or in combination with other crystals to strengthen the effects.

Clear Quartz

Smoky Quartz

Rose Quartz

MOONSTONE

Moonstone is known as 'the dreamer's stone'. It's connected with feminine issues, harmonising cycles of menstruation, fertility, pregnancy, birth and menopause. It's also useful for people who can feel overwhelmed in busy environments and crowds. Moonstone can deflect energy and improve boundaries. There's nothing to be gained from losing yourself.

Although moonstone energy is soft and caring it promotes bravery and empowerment. It can help you to take responsibility, boost courage, regain control and be true to yourself. Moonstone boosts intuition and emotional awareness and it's associated with happy new beginnings and self-worth.

Given as a wedding gift, moonstone is said to bless the couple with love, passion and fertility. In loving relationships, it helps with disconnection and silent retreat from arguments. When it comes to an ending, there is harmonious completion and wisdom that everything flows in natural cycles.

ATTRIBUTES:

Balance, intuition, feminine, harmony, birth, love, marriage.

PHYSICAL:

Heart, lungs, digestion, bladder kidney, reproductive organs, skin, hair.

CHAKRA:

Crown and third eye chakras.

CLEAR QUARTZ

Clear quartz has a reputation for being the "master healer." It's also known as rock crystal. As a high vibrational stone which amplifies energy, it's one of the most versatile and widely used crystals in the world. Clear quartz absorbs, transmutes and releases negative or low vibrations in all situations. Clear quartz can be paired with other stones to enhance their attributes, so it's a great additional stone to use.

Used in aura cleansing, clear quartz purifies, strengthens and energises where appropriate. Quartz is used to filter an over-stuffed mind and bring clear perspective. It sharpens focus, improves concentration, memory and revitalises both the mind and body. It's used for unwanted thoughts, worry, overthinking and fear. Clear quartz stimulates consciousness and intuition.

Although it strongly resonates with the crown chakra it works on balancing all of the chakras.

ATTRIBUTES:

Amplify, cleanse, purify, strengthen, rejuvenate, empower, clarity.

PHYSICAL:

All of the body.

CHAKRA:

Crown chakra.

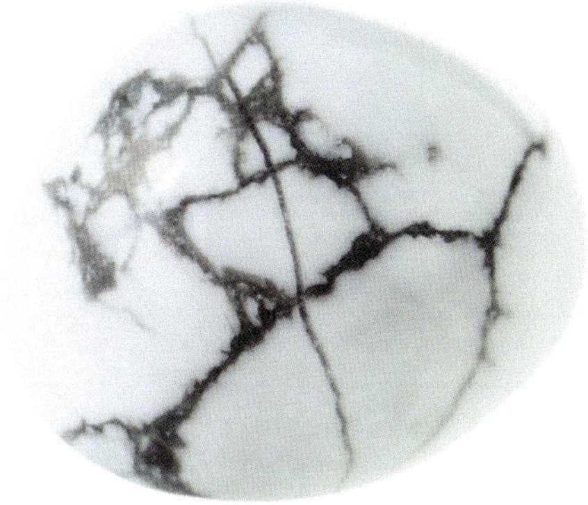

HOWLITE

Howlite is associated with positivity, inspiration and joy. It stimulates the smooth flow of positive energy through the body, recharging and balancing all aspects of your wellbeing. Howlite encourages co-operation between all living things as they are energetically connected, which means helping yourself is also helping others.

It's a benevolent stone which encourages open mindedness and the release of stress. It's an empowering stone, which is good for motivating you to rise to new challenges and prove that you are more capable than you imagine. Howlite draws energy through the top of your head which is dispersed throughout the body. It encourages you to make positive changes and go beyond limits. You can use howlite in meditation with the affirmation, 'old beliefs have no power over me now.'

ATTRIBUTES:

Inspiration, positivity, oneness, simplicity, peace, spiritual connection.

PHYSICAL:

Head, neck and all of the body.

CHAKRA:

Crown chakra.

SELENITE

Selenite is a purifying mineral rock which is widely used for dispelling negative energies and cleansing other crystals. It's also known as white gypsum. Selenite's superpower is that it does not need to be cleansed and it acts as a re-charging point, absorbing, transforming and releasing energies. Some people like to cleanse or recharge it anyway to make sure it is effective, so go with your gut instinct on this one. Selenite works on both people and the environment and it's a lovely crystal to have in your home.

Selenite is often used in meditation for calming the mind and stilling the body. It's a good crystal to enhance distant communication and improving bonds in relationships. It's used for fear and defensiveness, improving trust when appropriate.

Selenite is used to connect with the angels for protection and guidance, particularly guardian angels. It's important to always ask them for help, otherwise they'll honour your free will. Selenite can be used during the dark night of the soul, reassuring you that brighter days are coming. As a promoter of change, it's empowering, cleansing, forgiving, fortifying and rejuvenating. It can also be used to ease suspicion and paranoia.

ATTRIBUTES:

Cleansing, purifying, revitalising, empowering, intuition, guidance.

PHYSICAL:

Brain, immune system, bones, teeth, chest, cell renewal.

CHAKRA:

Crown chakra.

AMETHYST

Amethyst is considered a primary stone used for protection and purifying. This rich purple stone is a stress reliever and is associated with insight, wisdom and compassion, promoting sleep and dream recall.

Amethyst is said to be the best crystal for brain development in small children. It's used to calm fear of the unseen and dispels negative forces generated by your own mind such as fear of the dark. Amethyst helps to discharge low, depressive energies from others and the world in general. It works on self-esteem and particularly body image.

As an amplifier with a strong connection to the third eye chakra, it's often held in the hand during meditation to improve intuition and understanding of unseen realities and improving psychic development. It resonates with the crown chakra, which points upwards and connects to a higher reality for greater learning and understanding of spiritual existence.

Amethyst can bring renewed understanding of love and promote healing on a psychic level. It resonates with an altered state of being, used for manifesting, and grounding the body. Amethyst increases the positive flow of energy, raising vibrations and it's said to be the 'Ascension stone'. It's protective influence is good for travel, both physical and astral, and it's used by shamans for safe steady progress when making a journey.

ATTRIBUTES:

Relaxing, psychic gifts, calming, protection, purifying, grounding.

PHYSICAL:

Eyes, ears, nose, hormones, nervous system, sleep, metabolism.

CHAKRA:

Third eye and crown chakras.

SUGILITE

Sugilite is an uplifting stone, used for romantic love and attracting a partner. It's a very protective stone which is useful for sensitive empathic people who struggle with feeling the emotions of others.

Sugilite is used in divination, memory recall and spiritual guidance. Sugilite is said to help locate something which has been misplaced or lost. If memories of past events, heartache and trauma are triggered it can help you to release and heal the emotion. Sugilite filters out difficult past experiences, aids forgiveness and brings a fresh, positive perspective.

When your mind keeps going round and round – sugilite may help get to the root of the problem. Holding this stone during meditation can create a connection between the past and present, enabling transformation. Sugilite is a great stone for foresight of what lies ahead. It helps you know how to improve your energy, which ripples out and improves what you attract in.

ATTRIBUTES:

Love, foresight, forgiveness, protection, guidance, joy, comfort.

PHYSICAL:

Heart, lung, brain, circulation, nervous system.

CHAKRA:

Crown and heart chakras.

AMETRINE

Ametrine is a crystal for money and enlightenment. It's a combination of amethyst and citrine in one crystal, which holds the benefits of both stones. It blends together material and spiritual aspects and ideas. It promotes harmony between 2 people in a relationship, blending them together with loving energy. It can be used for finding meaning in everyday life. Ametrine stimulates the solar plexus and crown chakras, which is helpful for processing emotions with increased wisdom. Ametrine can be used to strengthen vitality, creativity, willpower and intuition. It can be used for letting go of anger, sadness, fear and stress, allowing you to move on and feel greater happiness again.

Ametrine resonates with the solar plexus chakra which revitalises, improves creativity and manifesting desires. It's connection to the crown chakra generates tranquillity and benefits depression. This unique stone strengthens the flow of energy and guidance on your life path.

ATTRIBUTES:

Prosperity, wellbeing, vitality, motivation, creativity, wisdom, strength.

PHYSICAL:

Blood, immune system, digestion, head, memory, stress.

CHAKRA:

Solar Plexus and crown chakras.

LABRADORITE

Labradorite is a carefree travellers stone for protection and finding a new path. It improves a pessimistic attitude and turns grey skies to blue. It can help you to see the magic in everyday life. Labradorite sharpens the eyes and the mind, eases doubts and reveals that all is actually well.

Insight can be gained that life is not as bleak and depressing as it may seem. Labradorite inspires fresh thought, independence and self-respect for all round wellbeing. It helps you let go, lifts your mood and shifts you from shadows. It's helpful for foresight during life changes. Labradorite helps you to heal from tough experiences with a happier, optimistic attitude.

Labradorite is used to ease dark night of the soul experiences and reassure you that there is no need to repeat it. It can be used for strength to overcome obstacles, fear and anxiety, freeing you to embrace new opportunities. Labradorite shows you that there is light at the end of the tunnel.

ATTRIBUTES:

Reassuring, transforming, relaxing, comforting, uplifting.

PHYSICAL:

Brain, eyes, ears, nervous system, neck, throat, shoulders.

CHAKRA:

Third eye and throat chakras.

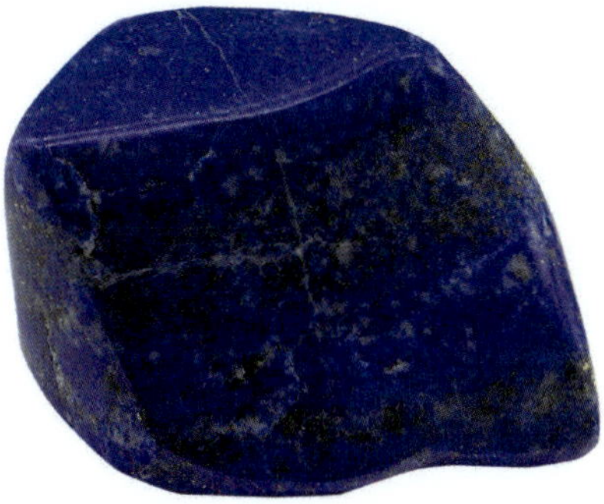

LAPIS LAZULI

Lapis lazuli is associated with reducing stress and calming the mind. It's so uplifting and it creates a refreshing, peaceful atmosphere in a room. It's used to support confidence especially if there is an event which involves performance or public speaking such as a wedding. It makes a thoughtful gift of 'something blue' for a bride-to-be.

Lapis lazuli's resonates with the third eye chakra. It's often used in jewellery so it's very wearable. This multi-functional crystal radiates cheerful, carefree energy. It's often small in size but big in strength, which means it's a great stone for carrying in your purse or pocket. Used in meditation it opens the mind to higher ideas and helps you to access infinite, loving supportive vibrations. Lapis is an ideal crystal for shyness, calming fears and improving focus.

ATTRIBUTES:

Support, confidence, peace, calm, communication, focus, perception.

PHYSICAL:

Spine, blood, immune system, throat.

CHAKRA:

Third eye chakra.

SODALITE

Sodalite is for self-expression and the courage to stand up for yourself. It calms the nervousness which causes people to talk too much and helps them to balance their expression. It's good for those who use their voice a lot, such as teachers, singers and performers, improving focus, intuition and genuine confidence.

Sodalite helps you to express and release what has been held in so that it can heal. It works on suppressed emotions which are harmful especially when anger turns inwards. Trauma and suppressed emotions can be held in the cells and effect mental and physical health

Use sodalite when someone has been putting on a brave face and the truth needs to surface. When pain has been silently borne, it can be released to the surface where healing can take place. It shines light on the shadows. Self-destructive feelings can be released and harmony restored. Sodalite generates the strength to overcome adversity. It's a lovely stone to give to a friend who has been strong for too long.

ATTRIBUTES:

Calming, reassuring, emotional expression, wisdom, courage.

PHYSICAL:

Brain, heart, neck, throat, immune system, adrenals, metabolism.

CHAKRA:

Third eye and throat chakras.

PEACOCK ORE

This beautiful multi-coloured stone brings positivity and prosperity. It promotes personal power and can be used for dealing with jealousy, criticism, insults and verbal negativity.

Peacock ore energy stimulates positive transformation, acceptance and self-love. It's known as a protective stone which acts like an invisible shield, offering the security to showcase your unique beauty and talents. It can be used to improve creativity, especially art and design skills. It eases doubt and brings confident focus on new projects.

Peacock ore is a type of pyrite, which resonates with the solar plexus, so it's useful for manifesting independence, prosperity and happiness. It's versatility helps balance and energise the other chakras too.

ATTRIBUTES:

Self-love, protection, prosperity, creativity, independence, success.

PHYSICAL:

Eyes, ears, throat, nervous system, stomach, heart.

CHAKRA:

All chakras and especially solar plexus and throat chakras.

TURQUOISE

Frequently used as a talisman by Native Americans, turquoise is a calming, purification stone and is known as a great healer. It's also known as a friendship stone and can be worn to create a comfortable atmosphere. Turquoise is used for exhaustion, mood swings and depression. It's frequency enhances creativity, wisdom and understanding that everything exists on many levels and healing of the mind and spirit is manifested in the body. As above, so below.

Turquoise is an uplifting, supportive stone for transformation and rejuvenation of every aspect of the body, mind and spirit. Turquoise improves self-awareness and understanding of what is needed to find greater peace, happiness and health.

Turquoise is often used as a good luck charm, for protection and balancing the emotions. It also connects with ancestral and family energy, bringing greater wisdom and support. Turquoise has a peaceful unifying energy which can be useful for disagreements and conflicts.

ATTRIBUTES:

Self-awareness, friendship, peace, honesty, unity, change, growth.

PHYSICAL:

Lungs, heart, neck, shoulders, thyroid, bones, immunity.

CHAKRA:

Throat chakra.

BLUE LACE AGATE

Blue Lace Agate brings hope, confidence and calm expression. It is a protective stone which is useful when domineering people and energies try to overwhelm your free will. Blue lace agate is a nurturing, calming stone which helps you to express your feelings. It's used for overcoming shyness and it's said to transform electromagnetic waves and purify harmful energy.

This soothing stone can help you to deal with stress, self-criticism, anxiety and panic. Agate is a positive and uplifting crystal which also comes in pink, black, yellow, blue, red, brown, grey and white. The colour of the stone corresponds with the chakra of the same colour. The blue lace agate in this picture, relates to the throat chakra, so it helps with all aspects of communication. It's empowering and great for tapping into your hidden strengths. It promotes courage to stand up for your beliefs.

ATTRIBUTES:

Confidence, calm, courage, communication, transformation.

PHYSICAL:

Lymphatic system, blood, circulation, throat, neck, shoulders, immunity.

CHAKRA:

Throat and crown chakras.

KYANITE

Kyanite helps resolve anger, calms the heart, soothes and heals the emotions. It's a soft yet powerfully effective crystal which is good for clearing old emotional energy that is stagnant and needs unblocked and released. It transforms lower energies, creating love from anger, trust from mistrust and brings out the beauty within. It can be used in meditation for releasing suppressed emotions, healing and finding greater peace.

Kyanite is useful for the intellect, learning new skills and abilities which is great if you are in education, training or personal development of any kind. It eases inhibitions, defensiveness, self-criticism and improves self-esteem.

Kyanite resonates with the moon and the emotions. Mystics and seers used kyanite to unblock and clear negative energies around them for accurate intuition, communication and speech.

ATTRIBUTES:

Transformation, communication, intuition, self-esteem.

PHYSICAL:

Neck, shoulders, throat, thyroid, blood pressure, pain, nerves, veins.

CHAKRA:

Throat chakra.

LARIMAR

Larimar is a manifestation stone, which holds the energy of gratitude, wealth, generosity and kindness. It is used for attracting opportunites and following your unique path. Larimar is a lovely stone to use with a gratitude journal. It helps transform negative beliefs such as fear of not having enough money, love or security which attracts what you don't want. It improves trust which encourages an abundance of all that you wish for, knowing your needs will be met.

Larimar increases joy and satisfaction. Its resonance with the throat chakra makes it good for projects linked to public speaking and teaching. It can be used to boost confidence and helps you to share your talents. It's helpful for replacing stress and worry with joy and light-heartedness. You can use larimar to change self-sabotaging beliefs and ease rigid thinking.

ATTRIBUTES:

Gratitude, manifestation, prosperity, flexibility, happiness.

PHYSICAL:

Bones, sinews, throat, glands.

CHAKRA:

Throat chakra.

APATITE

Apatite is associated with personal power, ambition and personal achievement. When you are frustrated, irritable and chronically tired, appatite helps you to rejuvenate. If your own needs have been neglected and you feel exhausted, you can use it for balancing and nurturing yourself. Apatite is useful in meditation for dealing with grief, guilt, anger and melancholy.

This stone comes in other colours but most commonly it's a blue/green stone which connects with the throat and heart chakras. It's used for hyperactivity, boosting creativity, expression, stability and bringing desires to reality.

You can use apatite when you wish to speak honestly, communicate ideas and have better motivation. It's used to improve dream recall and accessing the subconscious to find solutions and identify patterns.

ATTRIBUTES:

Nurturing, rejuvenating, motivating, harmonising, calming.

PHYSICAL:

Metabolism, ligaments, bones, teeth, head, brain, immunity.

CHAKRA:

Throat and third eye chakras.

ROSE QUARTZ

Rose quartz is the stone of love. This beautiful pink stone is known for being the most important crystal for attracting soul mates and twin flames. It encourages love to flourish, attracting matching loving energies. Its powerful for encouraging soft, gentle and magnetic healing vibrations. Rose quartz has pure loving life force energy that resonates with the heart. Rose quartz helps you to love yourself then you will attract another who also loves and values you in the same way.

Rose energy has always been associated with love and romance. It attracts love in all its forms, harmonising relationships with respect, trust and self-worth – ideal for improving your self-love. It's used to improve connections in relationships and can bring comfort during grief. It's a key stone for any crystal collection.

Rose quartz generates natural charm. It gives loving healing energy to those who ask for it. It's also good for establishing boundaries against destructive behaviours and helps during difficult times. It promotes kindness to yourself and to others. Rose quartz amplifies compassion and generosity of spirit to animals, humans and nature.

ATTRIBUTES:

Love, romance, compassion, peace, happiness, contentment.

PHYSICAL:

Heart, circulation, immune system, thymus, lungs.

CHAKRA:

Heart chakra.

RHODONITE

Rhodonite is a stone of compassion, love and emotional healing. If cracks appear in a relationship, it can be used for loving communication and soothing hurt feelings. If there has been dishonesty, disappointment, conflict, broken promises, half-truths or differing beliefs, rhodonite can bring transformation and rejuvenation.

Rhodonite links with the heart chakra, for finding solutions, inspiration and creating a fresh new perspective. It's used in meditation for resolving trauma, heart break and difficulty letting go at the end of a relationship or bereavement. It's used to ease grief and sooth the heart when coping with the death of a loved one and dealing with fear. It's helpful for finding peace amidst despair and sadness.

Rhodonite is also a stone of wisdom, gratitude and thankfulness for life lessons. It's also used for easing strained friendships and boundary setting.

ATTRIBUTES:

Contentment, joy, resilience, love, acceptance, hope, wisdom, gratitude.

PHYSICAL:

Heart, circulation, lung, liver, gallbladder.

CHAKRA:

Heart chakra.

PINK KUNZITE

Pink Kunzite is for unconditional love and sincere communication. It protects a vulnerable, open heart for safe and authentic expression. It can be overlooked as a protective stone, due to its soft loving vibration, but love dissolves all other things. Pink Kunzite is used for forgiveness and it's a great stone for cooling outbursts from rejection.

Pink Kunzite stimulates the pineal gland and third eye chakra, improving intuition and clarity. It can help you distinguish truth from dishonesty. If you feel you aren't being told the truth, pink kunzite will strengthen your ability to perceive what is not transparent. It's an excellent stone overcoming manipulation and heartbreak.

You can use it to connect to guides and angels. Just ask them to come close and feel their soft loving energy. Sit quietly, holding pink kunzite and notice tingles, temperature changes and how you respond to vibrations. It can boost self-awareness and inspired action.

ATTRIBUTES:

Joy, inspiration, communication, forgiveness, love, self-awareness.

PHYSICAL:

Pineal gland, heart, circulation, brain, sleep, memory.

CHAKRA:

Heart and third eye chakra.

RUBY ZOISITE

Ruby zoisite is a stone of rejuvenation, healing and optimism. It's used for vulnerability, fear, anxiety, grief and chronic illness. It instils hope, motivation and the ability to overcome fears. It lifts the mood which prevents negative thoughts jeopardising new opportunities and experiences. It eases self-sabotage, promotes confidence and assurance of success.

This is a supreme choice of stone for stubbornness and rigidity. It's helpful for planning and easing work burdens. Ruby zoisite soothes and strengthens the heart chakra and solar plexus chakra for optimism, clarity, planning and decision making.

Ruby zoisite helps clear obstructions and reveals new possibilities. It's used as a good luck stone for bringing positivity and new opportunities. It boosts foresight, keen judgement and intuition for making decisions, life changes, progressing careers, contracts and negotiations.

ATTRIBUTES:

Calming, transformation, strength, clarity, planning, decisiveness.

PHYSICAL:

Liver, gallbladder, pancreas, spleen, stomach, heart, eyes.

CHAKRA:

Heart chakra, solar plexus and crown chakra.

JADE

Jade is a wonderfully versatile stone which engenders love, trust and protection. Traditionally, jade was considered a deeply spiritual stone, often used in China for jewellery and carvings. It came to be known as 'the seekers stone'. A piece of jade was a traditional family heirloom in China, said to help develop skills and awareness, passing on wisdom and attributes to the next generation.

Jade is a spiritual gemstone which resonates with the heart and unites those who are like-minded. It bridges the physical and spiritual world and it's a way-shower for the discontented and broken-hearted. It's used to ease hostility and help peaceful communication. Jade is said to bring wisdom to enable you to see the bigger picture and heal what is broken. Jade stimulates clarity and wisdom, related to the circle of life. It resonates with re-birthing, rejuvenation and the natural life cycles. It can be used in meditation to ease grief and bring new beginnings from painful endings.

ATTRIBUTES:

Wisdom, love, protection, prosperity, gratitude, trust, success.

PHYSICAL:

Heart, brain, lungs, head, spine, hips.

CHAKRA:

Heart chakra.

AMAZONITE

Amazonite is a happy stone which zings with life and radiates care-free, relaxing energy. It was often used as a talisman in ancient times. Amazonite centres the mind and body. It instils positivity, strength, bravery and quiet courage. Amazonite is associated with using your consciousness to manifest your desires, realise your dreams and fulfil your heart. It raises intuition to a higher level of knowing what is pure, good and healthy for you.

Amazonite's frequency generates laughter and abundance of pleasure, love, empathy and understanding. The delicate colour of amazonite makes it a favourite for carvings and jewellery. It promotes healing for all of the chakras.

Amazonite encourages peace between partners, families, cultures and societies. It's used for finding common ground and similarities for better co-operation, oneness and union of groups with individual dynamics. It eases tension in conflicting groups who appear outwardly different.

ATTRIBUTES:

Soothe, relax, playful, care-free, peaceful, unifying.

PHYSICAL:

Hormones, heart, circulation, head, hair, nails, skin.

CHAKRA:

Heart chakra and crown chakra.

AVENTURINE

If you wish to create positive opportunities, abundance and prosperity, use green aventurine. It's beneficial for jealousy and stabilising the emotions. It's a stone for encouraging receptivity to love, joy and healing, improving self-worth and enabling heart-ache to heal.

When there are control issues, self-abuse and destructive patterns of behaviour, aventurine can be used to transform jealous, negative behaviour which sabotages happiness. Used in meditation, aventurine helps you to transform abusive situations, heartache, over-control, emotional fatigue, criticism and hatred.

Aventurine motivates you to take control of your life and eliminates any need to restrict yourself or others. It shows how letting go is not the same as abandonment which soothes neediness and insecurity. It draws scattered energy together so that you can independently follow your own path. You can fulfil your dreams without taking others with you. Aventurine helps you cut cords and let go; neither taking hostages nor being a hostage. Your life is yours to live. Let others go with the flow also.

ATTRIBUTES:

Strength, prosperity, independence, security, self-love, justice, courage.

PHYSICAL:

Heart, liver, gall bladder spleen, kidneys, immunity, chronic fatigue.

CHAKRA:

Heart chakra.

BLOODSTONE

The energetic power of this gemstone is determination, courage and motivation. It propels movement forward in challenging, fearful situations. Bloodstone is a warrior stone of strength and decisive action. It can be useful where choices affecting the head and the heart need to be made.

As its name suggests, bloodstone strongly resonates with the life-giving energy of the blood. It's a purifier and cleanser of negative vibrations and low energies, such as anger, despair, depression, anxiety and sadness. Bloodstone is known as a 'soul healer', which attracts healing and transformation. It clears a path and inspires action.

Bloodstone is a physically grounding stone which brings warmth, friendliness and fiery energy, for letting go of the past. It's used to overcome resistance and strengthen willpower. It helps the mind to go beyond what has gone before to enjoy new opportunities.

ATTRIBUTES:

Transformation, motivation, strength, wisdom, willpower, grounding.

PHYSICAL:

Heart, blood, spleen, liver, kidneys, muscles.

CHAKRA:

Heart and root chakras.

MALACHITE

Malachite is known as 'the stone of transformation'. It's an uplifting stone for vulnerability, fragility, love, heartbreak, anxiety and loss. It's used to balance suspiciousness, fear, shyness and stress. Malachite is great as a talisman for life changes, transformation and healing. It's a good stone for when you're running on empty and you're mentally and physically exhausted. Malachite helps you to give yourself what you need.

This rich green crystal has a happy vibration which lifts the mood, inspires problem solving and self-healing. It can be used to help resolve harsh feelings, restore broken friendships and release relationships which are unhealthy. In meditation it can help you to make life changes with confidence. It's used to clear the mind of doubt, stabilise anxiety from a hectic lifestyle. Malachite connects the heart and mind, enhancing decision making and authentic expression.

ATTRIBUTES:

Transforming, clearing, uplifting, calming, relaxing, balancing.

PHYSICAL:

Liver, gall bladder, heart, muscles, digestion, kidneys, reproductive system.

CHAKRA:

Heart chakra.

FLUORITE

Fluorite is a beautiful eye-catching stone for clarity and mental focus. It's also a protective, strengthening and restorative crystal, which can be used to deflect negative influences. Fluorite is a popular, versatile stone which can also be used for learning, memory enhancement and decision making. It's also used for confidence, relaxation, resilience and conflict resolution, particularly if power struggles are involved.

Fluorite is used to improve mental function and intuitive perception to see what is below the surface. It helps you to use all your senses, improves your ability to recognise hidden agendas with strength and determination to take back control. It resonates with the heart and third eye chakras and improves interpretation of gut feelings and psychic insights. On a mental level it's used for improving concentration and clearing brain fog. Some also find fluorite helpful in dealing with electromagnetic energies.

ATTRIBUTES:

Mental focus, clarity, calm, strength, decisive, resilience, intuition.

PHYSICAL:

Kidneys, heart, spleen, bones, teeth, throat, brain, memory.

CHAKRA:

Heart and third eye chakras.

PYRITE

Pyrite is a glittery stone which is associated with good luck, wealth and success. Although it's also known as 'fool's gold', there is nothing foolish about this stone, which is used to stimulate the brain, memory and intellect. It works on physical vitality and motivation towards personal success. Pyrite is also a protective stone which rejuvenates and balances.

Pyrite can be used in meditation to restore wellbeing from stress, burnout and overwhelming emotions. It calms excess energy and revitalises depletion, making it a good choice for stabilising the mind and body.

Pyrite has a phoenix-like energy and is a steady rejuvenator after stressful events. It can harmonise parent and child relationships, especially after pregnancy and birth if it feels like there has been a loss of closeness. Pyrite can be useful for strengthening emotional healing linked to abandonment, neglect or isolation. It soothes the adrenals and calms the fight-or-flight instinct.

ATTRIBUTES:
Wealth, success, energising, creativity, relaxing, grounding.

PHYSICAL:
Intestines, stomach, spleen, liver, blood, adrenals.

CHAKRA:
Solar plexus chakra.

GOLDEN TOPAZ

Golden topaz is a beautiful luminous amplifier of energy. It stimulates emotional healing, especially if giving too much of yourself has caused depletion and exhaustion. It helps reveal what has been hidden behind a brave face, such as resentment, anxiety, depression and sadness, which can be released for greater happiness.

Golden topaz can be used for self-care and dealing with emotions which haven't been fully processed and healed. It can ease defensiveness and the need to hide behind a mask, which allows hurt and pain to be transformed. Golden topaz helps you to let go of what you no longer need and discover a happier you, under layers of old negative emotions. It helps with feelings of security. It uplifts, purifies, amplifies positive energy and resonates with the solar plexus chakra.

ATTRIBUTES:
Purifying, uplifting, amplifying, balancing, inspiring.

PHYSICAL:
Digestion, spleen, pancreas, intestines, liver, lung, ribs, chest.

CHAKRA:
Solar plexus.

CITRINE

Citrine is a pale yellow quartz crystal which radiates sparkle, joy and enthusiasm. It's an energising stone which is used to boost confidence, optimism, warmth and motivation. Citrine is associated with mental processing, clarity and concentration useful for overcoming negativity, dejection, fear and loneliness.

Citrine is a great stone to use in meditation to soothe, relax and uplift the mind. It shines with sunny, happy energy. It acts as a transformer of low energy such as depression, apathy and despondency. Citrine is also associated with attracting wealth and improving finances. It's an auspicious crystal for attracting positive, fortunate outcomes in work and business, learning, improving your skills and personal development. Citrine can be used for problem solving and encouraging triumph over adversity.

ATTRIBUTES:

Happiness, optimism, warmth, reassuring, phobias, creativity.

PHYSICAL:

Stomach, spleen, pancreas, intestines, hormones, chronic illnesses.

CHAKRA:

Solar plexus.

AMBER

Amber is a 'nurse crystal' which nurtures and calms irritability. Amber is a lovely stone for convalescence. It's a sunny crystal which grounds and reassures. It lifts the spirits in a gentle, safe way without too much stimulation.

The magic of this stone truly exists in the ability to connect with the parts of yourself which need healed from chronic pain, illness, emotional pain, poor vitality and lack of will to go on. It generates strength and the resolve to be part of life. It's protective motherly vibration helps pull you back together when you feel scattered.

Hold an amber tumble stone in your hand and feel if it resonates with you. Be aware of your emotions and physical sensations. Amber is connected strongly with life changes; teenage issues, baby and child development stages, relationship issues, divorce and dying. It represents the cycle of life, and all its phases, birth and death, ending and renewal. It's associated with accepting mortality. Amber offers solid, transformational and nurturing energy during personal and physical growth.

ATTRIBUTES:

Nurturing, reassuring, stabilising, calming, grounding.

PHYSICAL:

Digestion, hormones, sex organs, skin, teeth, hair.

CHAKRA:

Solar plexus and sacral chakras.

SUNSTONE

Sunstone has a simple, uplifting, happy energy that shows you how to really enjoy life. Sunstone inspires opportunities, career advancement and provision of your material needs. The energy quality of this stone is closely linked with the solar power of the sun, it has the ability to shine in dark places and bring relief, hope and radiance. People who resonate with sunstone energy, light up a room with their presence. Sunstone encourages you to seek happiness and enjoy sensual pleasures. It helps and encourages you to discover what it is that really makes you happy.

Used in meditation, sunstone eases stress, anger, fear, worry, over-thinking and obsessive thought. Its warmth and optimistic energy relaxes tension, benefits fatigue and exhaustion. Sunstone encourages the flow of peace within you and empowers you to be the care-taker of your own pleasure, happiness and well-being.

ATTRIBUTES:

Charm, optimism, positivity, trust, sexuality, joy, pleasure.

PHYSICAL:

Stomach, spleen, intestines, metabolism, reproductive organs, fertility.

CHAKRA:

Sacral and solar plexus chakras.

CARNELIAN

Carnelian is a stone for fresh energy, new ideas and creativity. It inspires unshakeable confidence which elevates your self-esteem so you feel good just being you. Carnelian instils peace, resilience, radiance and trust, showing you nothing can dull your shine when bright energy is flowing within you.

Carnelian helps balance the ego, unblocks stagnant emotions and reveals your true self. If you have doubt, worry or fear, carnelian is a useful stone to wear or carry with you. It helps you to know when to trust, when to stay, when to go and when to heal. It can be used for patience, accepting divine timing, trusting fate and learning to trust your gut instincts.

Carnelian helps calm the urge to push ahead when it isn't time yet. It transforms apathy, helps release fears and attracts greater happiness.

ATTRIBUTES:

Confidence, self-esteem, patience, stamina, resilience.

PHYSICAL:

Stomach, spleen, intestines, reproductive organs, muscles.

CHAKRA:

Sacral chakra.

TIGER'S EYE

Tiger's eye is known for protection, strength and clarity of thought. It's often used as a talisman to enhance personal power and increase motivation. It doesn't get its name from it's rich golden brown colour, but because it holds the tiger's attributes of insight, patience and determination. It inspires clear decisive action and can be used for an overactive and worried mind.

Tiger's eye boosts courage to take action to secure what you want, particularly for family safety, home and material necessities. It sharpens your instincts and intellect. It can be helpful for working on worry and anxiety, helping you to see the things you worry about are not really problems at all. It helps you to trust your gut instincts around divine timing, when to take action and when to trust in fated events. Tiger's eye energy is grounding and calming when big changes are happening. It's a great warrior against injustice and helps you to let go of what is not in your best interests. It's reassures mothers not to doubt their instincts.

ATTRIBUTES:

Perception, judgement, instincts, bravery, trust, security.

PHYSICAL:

Head, eyes, kidneys, bladder, intestines, stomach, spleen, colon.

CHAKRA:

Solar plexus, sacral and root chakras.

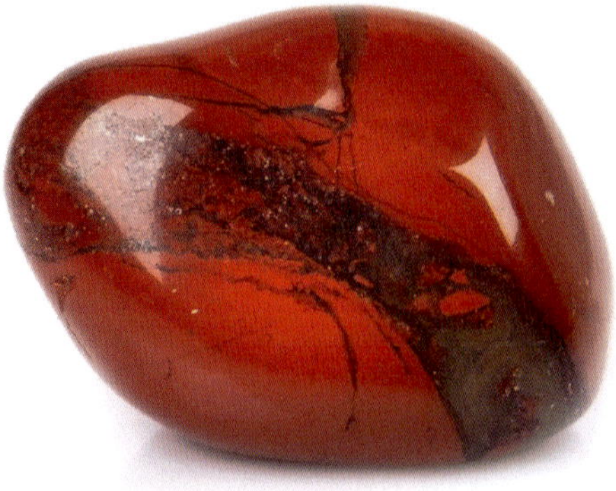

JASPER

Jasper is associated with great wisdom and is known as the 'seeker's stone.' Fun, laughter, creativity, dynamic charm and confidence are also associated with red jasper. It draws people together and it's great for keeping a positive environment when projecting ideas to groups.

Jasper is invigorating, boosts courage, confidence and mental agility. Used as a talisman, it gives protection from negativity and helps you to be authentic and find joy in life. It can be used to ease fear, recklessness, worry and compulsive behaviours. If success provokes jealously, this stone's protective energy is ideal. Jasper has a profound harmonising ability for uniting people in a common purpose and it's good for enhancing teamwork and strength of character.

Jasper has been widely used by healers and shamans who are strongly connected to the spirit world. It comes in a variety of colours and shades which generally resonates with the chakra of the corresponding colour.

ATTRIBUTES:

Joy, protection, confidence, consistency, passion, warmth.

PHYSICAL:

Sex organs, stomach, intestines, metabolism, blood, hormones.

CHAKRA:

Sacral and root chakras.

SMOKY QUARTZ

Smoky quartz is a stone of power, purity and strength. It can be used for worry, confusion and bad moods. If you're feeling gloomy it's surprising how quickly it can change by holding smoky quartz for a few minutes. It's also a grounding stone which is reassuring, warm, cleansing and welcoming. It's revered for being the strongest healer of the mind and heart, helping clear your way to being your best self.

Smoky quartz imparts security and serenity. It's a good match for using with other stones to enhance and ground their effects. It can show you how to enjoy life at a slower pace with greater trust and joy. It creates a homely, safe atmosphere and can be used to bring a warm, cosy feel to a room.

Smoky quartz can be used in meditation for depression, hostility, trauma, guilt and fear, transforming those energies and supporting anyone struggling with the past

ATTRIBUTES:

Purity, strength, power, warmth, serenity, grounding.

PHYSICAL:

Spleen, colon, abdomen, legs, adrenals, kidneys, bladder, fluids.

CHAKRA:

Root chakra.

OBSIDIAN

Obsidian is known as the 'stone of truth' and it's commonly used for protection and strength. It's stabilising and calming, allowing anything that has been hidden to come to the surface. It's used for environmental stress and can help to soothe a mind which is over-stimulated by chaotic environments, crowds or negative situations. Obsidian is the calm in the midst of a storm when there is too much activity around you.

Black obsidian, also called volcanic glass, is best known for being powerfully protective and absorbing all kinds of negativity including shock, anger, trauma, pain, criticism and jealousy. It can be worn as a talisman or used in meditation for resilience to stress and to avoid becoming depleted by other people's dramas and emotions.

You can use it regularly to strengthen positivity and help release emotional and karmic blockages. Obsidian resonates with the root chakra, so it works on fear, insecurity and vitality.

ATTRIBUTES:

Protection, patience, strength, calms, releases tension.

PHYSICAL:

Stomach, spleen, intestines, colon, liver, gall bladder, muscles, immunity.

CHAKRA:

Root chakra.

GARNET

Garnet is known as the 'stone of commitment' and it's often used in jewellery. It's a robust gemstone which is said to attract love, passion and devotion. It generates trust and security that all is well, soothing emotional pain and sadness.

It's reassuring energy brings together partnerships, family, home and stability. Garnet reinforces your courage to ask for what you need. It works on issues related to love, passion, food, shelter, wealth, community and life sustaining necessities. On an emotional level, garnet is associated with healing grief, sadness and fear, giving you the opportunity to change and let go of old behaviour patterns.

Garnet enhances sincere communication with friends, family and lovers. The reassuring energy of this crystal attracts positive support and wisdom. It also links spiritually with the ancestors, so if you lack direction, it can attract positive guidance.

ATTRIBUTES:

Support, commitment, passion, trust, wisdom, security, contentment.

PHYSICAL:

Muscle strength, spinal column, cell growth, bones and ligaments.

CHAKRA:

Root chakra.

HAEMATITE

Haematite is used for enhancing confidence, willpower and courage. It's helpful for timidity, self-esteem, improving focus, uplifting and calming the mind. Haematite can help with producing ideas and improving self-awareness. It's grounding frequency can help a flighty mind, anchoring logical thoughts for resolving problems and financial planning.

Haematite is associated with memory, learning, forming ideas and realistic solutions. It's useful for harnessing new opportunities, establishing and attaining goals. It calms nervousness and generates practical, logical thinking. It's useful for when you feel your head is in the clouds and you need to focus on the job in hand. Haematite is a steely metallic stone which can be black, reddish brown, grey or silver which is often used for jewellery.

ATTRIBUTES:

Calming, protection, confidence, willpower, courage, ideas, logic.

PHYSICAL:

Blood, veins, reproductive organs, kidneys, bladder, legs, ankles feet.

CHAKRA:

Root chakra.

TOURMALINE

Black tourmaline is a protective and purifying stone which attracts positive energy.

Historically, tourmaline was known as a magical stone because of it's protective influence. It is used for stress, adrenal fatigue, fear and inflexibility. It's a key stone for transforming negativity and protection. It can help you to deal with anything which has held you back. It generates forgiveness and attracts new opportunities for happiness into your life.

If sticking too rigidly to old beliefs has prevented your progress, tourmaline can help you release the fear of letting go. It's associated with opening up to receive love and moving on from the past. It's also used for grief, self-criticism, depression and worry which can weaken vitality. Tourmaline generates compassion, gentleness and willingness to show affection.

Tourmaline is a great multi-functional stone to have in your crystal collection which many people can benefit from.

ATTRIBUTES:

Protection, transformation, grounding, cleansing, calming.

PHYSICAL:

Chronic health issues, legs, muscles, veins, tendons and injuries.

CHAKRA:

Root chakra.

Crystals For Your Wellbeing

Anger	*Black tourmaline, selenite, ametrine, kyanite, fluorite.*
Apathy	*Garnet, apatite, golden topaz, clear quartz, smoky quartz.*
Anxiety	*Fluorite, amethyst, smoky quartz, haematite, labradorite, malachite, obsidian, black tourmaline.*
Balance	*Agate, jasper, smoky quartz, haematite, moonstone, amber.*
Calming	*Haematite, tiger's eye, howlite, smoky quartz, selenite, pink kunzite.*
Clarity	*Clear quartz, turquoise, fluorite, golden topaz, tiger's eye.*
Cleansing	*Amethyst, selenite, ametrine, clear quartz, black tourmaline.*
Compassion	*Rhodondite, howlite, pink kunzite, rose quartz.*
Communication	*Labradorite, pink kunzite, lapis lazuli, turquoise, sodalite, larimar.*
Confidence	*Carnelian, sunstone, lapis lazuli, peacock ore, kyanite, tiger's eye, haematite.*
Courage	*Bloodstone, tiger's eye, tourmaline, turquoise, sodalite, jasper.*
Creativity	*Ametrine, carnelian, apatite, citrine, aventurine.*
Decisiveness	*Ametrine, fluorite, tiger's eye, bloodstone, ruby zoisite.*
Depression	*Smoky quartz, selenite, obsidian, labradorite, tourmaline, citrine.*
Fatigue	*Howlite, apatite, pyrite, golden topaz, amber, fluorite, jasper.*
Fear	*Garnet, sodalite, selenite, blue lace agate, pyrite, amber, bloodstone.*
Forgiveness	*Tourmaline, sugilite, golden topaz, selenite, pink kunzite, amethyst.*
Good luck	*Pyrite, aventurine, jade, peacock ore, citrine.*
Gratitude	*Larimar, rhodonite, clear quartz.*
Grief	*Apatite, tourmaline, ruby zoisite, rhodondite, obsidian.*
Grounding	*Tourmaline, amber, obsidian, garnet, carnelian, smoky quartz.*
Heartache	*Pink kunzite, sugilite, rose quartz, rhodonite.*

Hope	*Citrine, sunstone, ruby zoisite, selenite, amethyst, labradorite.*
Impatience	*Howlite, amazonite, tiger's eye, obsidian, garnet, smoky quartz.*
Intuition	*Amethyst, lapis lazuli, labradorite, moonstone, sodalite, selenite.*
Jealousy	*Aventurine, malachite, selenite, peacock ore, obsidian.*
Joy	*Amazonite, pink kunzite, larimar, jasper, sunstone.*
Life changes	*Selenite, kyanite, bloodstone, malachite, amber.*
Love	*Rose quartz, moonstone, garnet, rhodondite, sugilite, malachite.*
Manifesting	*Amethyst and garnet used together. Larimar, jade.*
Motivation	*Red jasper, ametrine, pyrite, carnelian, smoky quartz.*
Negativity	*Tourmaline, haematite, smoky quartz, obsidian, howlite, sunstone.*
Over-thinking	*Haematite, amber, blue lace agate, fluorite, aventurine, sunstone.*
Peace	*Howlite, turquoise, blue lace agate, ametrine, pink kunzite, amazonite.*
Positivity	*Clear quartz, sugilite, howlite, labradorite, peacock ore, agate.*
Prosperity	*Citrine, pyrite, peacock ore, larimar, jade, aventurine, amazonite, ametrine.*
Protection	*Selenite, amethyst, sugilite, jade, fluorite, obsidian, tourmaline, fluorite.*
Relationships	*Malachite, selenite, rose quartz, rhodondite, ametrine, pink kunzite, moonstone.*
Relaxation	*Amethyst, howlite, sugilite, lapis, sodalite, apatite, malachite.*
Security	*Carnelian, rhodondite, jade, bloodstone, tiger's eye, garnet.*
Self-esteem	*Rhodondite, moonstone, howlite, kyanite, tiger's eye, turquoise.*
Self-love	*Rose quartz, amethyst, peacock ore, aventurine, pink kunzite.*
Sleep	*Fluorite, moonstone, blue lace agate, tourmaline, amber, amethyst.*
Stress	*Haematite, amethyst, larimar, pyrite, sunstone, sodalite, obsidian.*
Success	*Jade, pyrite, citrine, carnelian, clear quartz, smoky quartz.*

Printed in Great Britain
by Amazon

35047592R00035